ENZO RAFFA

S. GIMIGNANO

The Town with beautiful towers

GUIDE-BOOK
ART AND HISTORY

Edizioni GIANCARLO BOLDRINI - S. GIMIGNANO

PRINTED IN ITALY · UMBRIAGRAF · TERNI

AIR VIEW

*Seen from afar, the town seems inaccesible. Go[...]
up from the Poggibonsi road, which is the most tra[...]
cated, the towers lose their perspective and get do[...]
till disappearing among the olive trees. The brown[...]
very leaves increases the silence around red br[...]
walls. Seen from the Certaldo road, the town is m[...]
braggart. Towers are as straight as halberds. Be t[...]
rain wet or sun burnt, they always keep the very sa[...]
colour and maintain the same soleliness of the bl[...]
cypresses of these places.*

2

CISTERNA'S SQUARE

Thereafter, we do not see the town any longer and its doors open on streets anciently paved. Here and there houses whose roofs almost touch each other. Above, a narrow stripe of sky leads from Porta San Giovanni or from Porta San Matteo to the Cathedral Square. And here, in a space enlarging at a bell toll, a strange sensation of safety wraps our soul. Since 1214 San Gimignano promised «immunity» to those who were coming to the castle.

ARCH OF BECCI AND CUGNANESI

Between History and Legend

The origins of San Gimignano are very ancient and sink in the colourful tales of legend. These hills were certainly occupied by Etruscan people as it is testified by hypogea and urns discovered within and outside the town. A few pieces are now diplayed in the
Town Hall. After the Etruscans, the district under the municipality
of Volterra showed signs of life in the villages and the hamlets of
Collemuccioli and Cellole as well as within the walls.

It is part of the legend the place where San Gimignano had to be
built by Silvio, a young Roman who seems to have come here along
with his friend Muzio. Both involved in the conspiracy against Cati-
lina they rushly escaped and stopped in the Valdelsa; here, attract-
ed by the beauty of the place, they would have built two castles,
those of Silvia and of Muzio on top of two nearby hills. Muzio changed its name in Mucchio (a place bearing this name and having its history is still existing in the countryside of San Gimignano)
and Silvia became Silva or Castle of the Selva.

The names still pertaining to a few atreets such as Via del P
nello, Via Quercecchio, Via Piandornella, probably bear indicati
of trees sorrounding, far ago, the castle just likely it is today s
rounded by olive and vine trees. Following the legend which wa
to cover with glory its obscure origin, Silvia would have beco
San Gimignano in honor and thanks to the Saints Bishop from N
dena, by the same name, who would have liberated the castle fr
King Attila's siege in the year 450. Other personages, mentioned
history, seem to have been at San Gimignano; among them, De
derius, King of Longobards, and finally Charlemagne. It is cert
that Attila, the wild leader of Huns, who was in Italy in 452, did
go through Tuscany and probably poets like Ciaccheri and Lu
mistook him with Totila, King of Goths who devasted the Flore
ne territory, Attila is being mistaken with Totila. A painting, prese
ly in the Basilica sacristy, is dedicated to Attila's legendary sie

King Desiderius too never came to San Gimignano, even if
tower-house at Via S. Matteo is called Palace of King Desideri
We could, possibly, have some probabilities as far as Charlemag
visit is concerned. The great Emperor lived at Villamagna, near V
terra, in 774. In 786 he celebrated Christmas in Florence. It is no
be excluded that during his permanence in Tuscany, he pass
through San Gimignano.

Of all these stories and suppositions, based on a compreher
ble popular vanity, the most reliable version is that San Gimigna
started to really mean something during the sixhundred and its
ry first origins are tied up with Longobards invasion. Longobar
who came from Eastern Europe, came to Italy in 568. Their inc
sions, lasted up to 774, changed many features in the life of ru
populations who were compelled to gather on the hills nearby th
fields. It has been ascertained that as far as San Gimignano is c
cerned, one of the Longobards initiative was decisive. For milit
reasons, they did not want to use the Via Aurelia and its surro
dings near the Byzantine territories and therefore marked out
Via Francigena or Francesca or Romea. A tract of such way,
most important way of communication between West Europe a
Rome, in the Middle Ages, is still crossing San Gimignano fror
gate to the other, going over the hill through the Cathedral squa
Little by little, on top of the hill, it was begun the construction
pilgrim hospices, hotels for travellers and merchants shops, pr
te houses, churches. The Via Francigena meant the way of co
merce and welfare for about one thousand years, that is to say
a period during which San Gimignano was founded, expanded a
declined.

It was Cosimo I of the Medici who ordered to stop its expansi
forbidding in 1563 the Commune «to allocate even the sligh
amount for any need, be it sacred or profane». This prohibition h
dered any further development of the town with its walls, its so
res, its churches, its towers.

Out of legend these are the starting points of its history.

O'S STREETAND CISTERNA'S SQUARE

CISTER SQUARE - Night view

Before the Year 1000

Almost on top of the hill called Montestaffoli (or mount Asto
this name probably takes us back to facts and personages pert
ing to barbarian invasions), we find a church dedicated to St. l
colò, and remains of other habitations and activities. Almost t

**PANORAMA
FROM MONTESTAFFOLI'S FORTRESS**

date back to the beginning of the sevenhundred, the century of
Charlemagne. The contours of the apse, later incorporated to the
present Basilica, have recently been brought to light. They show
that the ancient Church, built on a lower level, had also a different

9

orientation, as it had the back to another village, built quite near it, but on a lower level, on a steep hill over the country. It was a to ered castle, erected on the palce where at present is the prison. (the 30 of August 929, the King of Italy Hugh of Provence gave th castle to the Bishop of Volterra, Adelardo. The castle, called in t donation act «Mount of the Tower», included the house of the shop as well as a Church dedicated to St. Stephen, called St. S phen in the Castle, or St. Stephen in «canòva». (The «canòva» wa warehouse used for corn storage). We had thus a village and a stle (castrum in mediaeval Latin) linked by a transverse road to \ Francigena (presently Via del Castello) having at the beginninc draw-bridge. (This is the reason whi a Church built in the 13th ce tury at the end of the bridge is still called St. Lawrence the bridge).

Little by little the two villages became larger and joined ea other reaching the first ring of walls enclosing the castle in t group of houses and palaces from Porta dei Becci and Cugnan to the Arch of the Chancery. The first ring was built at the end the 10th century.

From the very beginning San Gimignano was under the jurisc tion of the Bishop of Volterra. This latter ancient powerful town s ce the Etruscan period (6th century B.C.) had power over the lar territory running from the chalk cliffs of its hills to the beginning Mount Maggio in the green Elsa valley. King Hugh's donation sa tioned politically the presence of Volterra in the history of San mignano, a history of wars and revenges until San Gimignano me under the power of Florence. These events happened in 1: but at San Gimignano there is today a Church belonging to the shop's See of Volterra.

COMMUNAL MUSEUM - Dante's Hall: Hunting scene (detail)
Sienese School. 1290

10

COMMUNAL MUSEUM · Dante's Hall: **Hunting scene** (detail)
Sienese School. 1290

After the Year 1000

The most meaningful dates during the first part of the year one-thousand are neither many nor very important. In 1056 the Florentine Synod presided by Pope Victor II proclaimed the «plebane» Church a «Propositura» or Canony Church (plebane was called a church having the baptismal font). Pope Paschal II in 1104 ordered the people of San Gimignano to be faithful, that is subject to the jurisdiction of Volterra: «Today and for ever they have to remain under the Volterran Church». The papal recall shows the sign of the first disagreements. Next year San Gimignano placed itself under the protection of Countess Mathilde; she was a sweet and proud patron of Tuscany and her name, changed in Contessa or Tessa was for almost two centuries the one preferred by Tuscan women. In 1107 Countess Mathilde taking advantage of the devotion the town paid to her, confirmed the decree of Pope Paschal. In the following years the jurisdiction of the Bishop of Volterra became stronger and stronger and expanded beyond the castle to the nearby countries. As a consequence there were no families of a count in San Gimignano. On the contrary, there were minor feudatory families who paid obedience and taxes to the Bishop. The Castles

whose possession cost so much blood were those of Monte, Cas
glia, Ulignano, Fosci, Monteaugutolo, Piccena, Santa Cristina
Castelnuovo (today Castelsangimignano together with the pari
territory of San Gimignano and Cellore now Cellole) was direc
subject to the Bishop. Other Castles, such as those of Pulicciar
Mucchio, Villa Castelli, San Benedetto, Collemuscioli, San Quiri
and Pancole, Castelvecchio were governed by the Bishop of Volt
ra through the help of «Vicedomini» and «Castaldi» (farmers).
this dark period we remind a few Volterran Bishops whose histo
is interlaced with that of San Gimignano: Guido who in 1052 orga
zed the justice taking upon himself full discretional powers to su
a point as to be able to decide «quarrels by duels»; Ruggero wl
had strong strifes with his soldiers; Oldamaro who in 1139 purch
sed from Count Ranieri Pannocchieschi (the first of the family
bear this name) and from his wife Subilia the territories of their C
stle in Fosci.

The first attempt to act out of the Bishop's authority came out
1129 on the occasion of a war againt the Castle of Casaglia whi
San Gimignano tried to conquer. There is a date of a particular i
portance to be reminded during the second period of history.
1148 Pope Eugene III compelled by political reasons to esca
from Rome to Florence, went to San Gimignano and consecrat
the new Parish Church (the one still existing). The presence of tl
Pope and of his court in a castle so far from the Holy See was
sign of the progress of San Gimignano.

COMMUNAL MUSEUM · Dante's Hall: Hunting scene (detail)
Sienese School, 1290

PANORAMA
FROM MONTESTAFFOLI'S FORTRESS

From the Year 1150 to the Beginning of the Thirteenth Century

In 1150 the election of Bishop Galgano raised the Volterran Episcopate to the acme of temporal power. Larger and larger territories and feudal rights went to his hands. The territory under the Bishop's jurisdiction covered a country going from the Tyrrhenian sea to the Elsa river. But the town of Volterra did not want to continue to be submitted to the Pannocchieschi family who wished to render hereditary the episcopal office. At the peak of his power in 1170 Galgano was stabbed at the Cathedral door. Afterwards San Gimignano realizing that the Bishop government was becoming weak, started its role of free commune.

A free commune meant above all to act automomously both the political and commercial fields. Because of the many difficulties arisen in this role, it was a tendency more than a reality. However San Gimignano people showed astonishing gifts of tenacity and capability. From this moment, until the half of 1300, the town history is an inextricable confusion of fights both exterior and interior. When the time came, is a tangled muddle of intestine and internal wars. People fighted against everybody, but under the influence of Florence the tendency of the free Commune was Guelph. The jealousy of Ghibelline families stirred up trouble. This is also the period during which trade spread all over a space large also for today's communications.

Trade expansion was alive and florid for almost two hundred years. Oil, wine, corn, leathers had their natural endless sources the surrounding territories. Mules and asses made long processions in and out San Gimignano walls, just like described in the celebrated fresco by Lorenzetti in Siena. One of the activities which gave rich and quite easy gain, was that of coachmen; they joined a corporation realizing a system of mutual help, just like at our days.

But it was the trade itself that brought the name of San Gimignano to Poggiobonsi, Siena, Lucca, Pisa, Sardinia, Genoa, Naples Messina and Milan as well as at Venice. Outside of Italy to Acri, Tunis, Alexandria, France, to the large Provençal market and to the Champagne fairs, to Marseille. Merchants from San Gimignano went, during the first half of the 13th century to Syria. The trade saffron, a plant whose dried flowers were employed to dye cloth was extremely thriving. The welfare consequent to trade expansion, gave a strong development to the city growth. On the ridge of the hills where the Via Francigena went up and down, many buildings were quickly erected. Outside the first wall ring, the boroughs of San Giovanni and San Matteo were built and at the beginning of the 13th century they were protected by a second ring walls.

But let's come back to politcal events which are mostly war events. From the difficulties of Volterra, San Gimignano tries to large its sovereignty over the nearby castles, formerly belonging Volterra's Bishop. Thus, in 1169, noblemen and squires of Casaglia and Montalto submitted «spontaneously» to the Commune of San Gimignano. The same thing did in 1199 the lords of Castle Della Pietra who, two years before, had sworn the same loyalty to Volterra. It was just during this year, that San Gimignano's independence strengthened.

From this year on people of San Gimignano signed pubblic acts without the Bishop's tutelage. Here are the names of the first few consuls who governed the town: Galganetto di Jeno, Pagano Gradaloni, Ardingo di Alberto, Enrichetto di Francesco. The judicial power was in the hands of the Rectors whose appointment pertained to the Bishop. The administration of justice was the last to escape from Volterra's jurisdiction: as a fact San Gimignano did much to render it independent; polemic and seditious as they were people perhaps preferred to be judged by strangers. The deliberative power pertained to two different councils: the secret and the general or public. The former was generally formed by 50 members, the latter was much more numerous. This system compelled many families to take responsibility of public affairs. On some occasions of communal life, people had recourse to public general voting. At the top of the power was a Podestà who performed the duties of modern president of the republic. Formerly this appointment was exceptional, but later on it became customary. The first Podestà was Messer Maghinardo Malevolti of Siena. Since 12.. this charge was always given to a foreigner who had no connections with local interests and could thus be a right arbitror among the various families. During his office the Podestà was accompanied by a judge and a public notary. His person was protected by lifeguard called «berrovieri». All these persons formed the «family» of the Podestà while the actual parents or relatives were to stay far away during the time he was in charge. Firstly such a charge was lasting one year according to the Florentine procedure, but the period could be extended. Since 1279 the charge last six months. At San Gimignano the Podestà could not accept either dinner invitations or donations from anybody, not could make presents to anyone. Since 1241 many Sangimignanese persons were asked to become Podestà or People Captains in Tuscany and outside. According to 1255 and 1268 statutes, there were other charges like that of Town Major, ambassador, public crier, night watchman, night bell ringer, day bell ringer, town walker or toll collector. There was also a doctor surgeon in this small state that made of its autonomy the main reason of freedom and where artisan activities flourished as a service to the person as well as to the community.

EVA'S CRATION · Bartolo di Fredi (1356) · **Church of the Collegiata**

CREATION OF MAN (Bartolo di Fredi) Year 1356 · Collegiate Church
CREATION OF THE WORLD (Bartolo di Fredi) Year 1356 · Collegiate Church

The Thirteenth Century
an Iron Century

The new century starts with the first sally of San Gimignano into a regional field, side by side with Siena and Florence. In the vicinity of Certaldo on the hills famous for their production of oil and wine, rose the town of Semifonte. Such was the ambition of its founders that they intended to eclipse Florence and gave rise to the saying: «Florence stand aside, Semifonte is now a city». Opposed interests of the neighbouring towns and castles formed around the walls of Semifonte. Siena, for instance, was looking with a certain interest to the quick growth of Semifonte which could possibly stop the expansion of Florence towards the Valdelsa. Semifonte is Ghibelline, i.e. belongs to the Emperor's party while Florence is Guelph. The war against Semifonte started in 1202 and was a continuous intrigue of alliances and betrayals; at the end, however, Semifonte was completely destroyed. Till a few years ago we did not even know where the exact place of this promising town was, so deeply had it been destroyed: now it has been discovered the perimeter where the surrounding walls were standing, but nothing more. The castle of Fosci too was completely destroyed after its lords Sigerio and Antiochio, had become rebels, taking advantage of social troubles oc-

curred in 1204 after the war against Semifonte. Of the stro
Fosci's castle we have only the name of the moat that conveys t
water of Cornocchio to the river Elsa. The following year the war
made against the Ghibelline Siena because of the help it gave S
mifonte against Florence. But under the towers there is no peac
A few families, the richest ones, tried to impose their dominati
over the free Commune through the reappointment of commandi
situations. The popular sense of freedom reacted and the Coun
stated that nobody can be elcted Podestà before five years pa
the previous election.

The families involved had recourse to the Bishop of Volterra w
in 1217 repealed the decree. This intervention provoked politi
factions. The families of Gregorio and Cugnanesi drew upon th
hatred and feud. Two other families, the Ardinghelli and the Salv
ci, famous for trade welfare, fought one against the other for t
and other occurrences. From 1212 to 1235 with a few armistic
the war started against Volterra, aim of the ancient hatred of S
Gimignano. The Bishop-Count Pagano of the well known Pann
chieschi family wanted to regain San Gimignano that took
arms. The ups and downs of war were entangled. The position
the Blshop of Volterra was difficult in his own town as people tr
to get rid of him. The clergy itself and the priests of the Cathed
were against the Bishop. San Gimignano offered Pagano its h
and hospitality in 1213 when the struggle between the Bishop a
Volterra reached its acme because of the exploitation of the Vol
ran salt mines at Pomarance. Matters seemed to become smoot
thanks to the intermediation of Pope Innocent III who threaten
to transfer the Bishop's see. It is the time of St. Francis of Ass
and more than ever we can appreciate the value of the Saint's
ger work for peace, preaching in the towns of Umbria and Tusca
all more or less burnt by overwhelming fever for hatred and rev
ge. Meanwhile the hate between the Bishop and the people of V
terra stirred up again. Emperor Frederick II took part in the str
gle. San Gimignano backed the Bishop against Volterra obeying
the Emperor's orders given through the Bishop as his power v
only apparent. In fact the Bishop needed San Gimignano to co
nue the war. In 1227 a point of arrival during these fights was
armistice signed through the mediation of the Sienese Podes
The years to come saw important changes. The Bishop turn
against San Gimignano after having discovered that its homa
was only formal. San Gimignano besieged the castle of Gamba
where the Bishop took refuge, but was defeated. However also
victory of the Bishop was a defeat. Pagano who wielded better
sword than the Mass-book, entrused himself to the hands of S
Gimignano to escape those revengeful of Volterra. The expec
peace was this time obtained through the mediation of Flore
which took advantage of this event to extend its influence over
nearby town that was progressing too fast. The presence of Flor
ce was never completely disliked by San Gimignano because
strength was too little, but above all because San Gimignano
well up with Florence for trades, handicraft and art and for a
tain spiritual harmony.

In 1236, only one year after the exhausting war against Volte
San Gimignano fought with Florence against Pistoia where m
Ghibellines received hospitality, and was ready to fight also for
pe Gregory IX against Emperor Frederick II. During the previ
years a few knights from San Gimignano had taken part in the C
sades. Amongst these knights, Sir Gradalone, who taken priso
at Damiata was liberated after some time and upon his return
ceived great honors. 1260 is the year of the battle of Montaperti.
the 4th of September, south of Siena, on the hill facing Val d'Ar
the Guelphs of Florence and San Gimignano clashed with the C
bellines of Siena and Florence. In the vineyards, red and white
pes were ripening. The country was becomng yellow for an e

Fall. Farmers, fearing the war, had locked up their herds. Swords and lances sparkled in the silence of clay landscape. The clear water of Arbia was red with blood as wrote Dante in his «Divine Comedy». The Guelphs were defeated. It might be the end of Florence, but Farinata degli Uberti, the winner, defended the town with so much vigour that also San Gimignano was safe. The major representatives of Guelph party, Pellari, Torri, Mangeri, Useppi, Ardinghelli escaped. Ghibelline's flag took the place of the Guelph but the Guelphs did not delay to fight against Lucca which was the sole Tuscan city remained faithful to the Guelphs. At Lucca, San Gimignano troops were commanded by Farinata's son, Azolino degli Uberti. During the battle of Colle in Val d'Elsa, in 1269 also reminded by Dante in his «Divine Comedy», there was a complete overturning. At the beginning of June, when the fields were full of ripe corn, the Guelph army cancelled the defeat of Montaperti and a prosperous Tuscan town, the Castle of Poggiobonzio (today Poggibonsi) was completely destroyed. Built on the hill dominating the torrent Staggia, Poggiobonizio was a stronghold with high walls having inside fountains and statues and every surrounding hamlet had its church therein. Those who were not killed went into exile to Borgo Maturi, a borough with some stables, shops and money-changers, which became the present town.

The years to come were years of fights, under the Guelph and Ghibelline flags. San Gimignano was inclined to be Guelph but not to the extent of accepting Pope's domination. From 1239 there was a change in the tendency, consequent to the diplomatic actions of Pandolfo Passanella, the Emperor's captain general. Guelphs were banished from San Gimignano and two families the name of which is still tied to two of the most beautiful towers, Ardinghelli (Guelph) and Salvucci (Ghibelline) fought one aginst the other involving the whole population in the struggle. Notwithstanding the temporary Ghibelline domination, in 1243, Bishop Pagano, from the altar of Propositura, excommunicated the Emperor Frederick II and all those persons who, at San Gimignano, were members of the Ghibelline party; among these persons almost all the clergy backed the Emperor. However the excommunication became effective only after the Emperor's death in 1250. The Guelphs came back to the town but San Gimignano was not to know peace, but only fratricide struggles, leaving fiery signs on the hards stones of towers and walls. Notwithstanding all this, in 1253, San Gimignano lent the Bishop 3800 Lire that were never returned.

The last three decades of 1200 are equal to the previous ones. San Gimignano fought against Volterra, Guelph families against Ghibelline families. There was also a government formed by Guelphes and Ghibellines, but it lasted short. The battle of Benevento in 1266 put an end to the Ghibellines as a national power. The following year the government of San Gimignano went back to the Guephs even if a third of the councillors were Ghibelline. Meanwhile the Bishop of Volterra did not renounce the rule of San Gimignano by that time a many-towered town (but the number of towers did not reach 72 as was told later on).

When the opportunity offered the occasion, people went out of their walls to interfere with the affairs of the neighbours, of the Emperor and of the Pope. Consequently San Gimignano made war against Colle and Poggibonsi, that hindered the traders, by imposing too heavy taxes. San Gimignano fought also against Castelfiorentino, against Arezzo where the Ghibelline front had moved. And at last the battle of Campaldino, on the 11 June 1289, the third of the great battles of Tuscany and San Gimignano at the end of the century. But before the century was over there were troubles with the clergy. Priests were bearing heavy taxes. To protest against this treatment they went away carrying with them the sacred furnishings. The town was compelled to hire a priest for four pennies a day. This situation lasted for two years. In 1292 a Bishop

SALVUCCI TWIN TOWERS

CATHEDRAL SQUARE · PODESTA'S PALACE

of Ardinghelli's family (Scolaio, Archishop of Tiro and Arborea Sardinia) brought again peace and the fugitives came back to gre satisfaction of everybody. This event is reminded in a painting the Town Hall.

CATHEDRAL SQUARE · Salvucci's Towers Hall and Rognosa Tower

After
the Fourteenth Century

The new century started with the embassy of Dante Alighieri on the 8th of May 1300. The great poet spoke in the Town Hall to the general council summoned by the Podestà Mino dei Tolomei. It was an important moment, to be remembered as one of the happiest events of the city. Dante asked the strengthening of the Guelph league and San Gimignano accepted. From then on San Gimignano was always involved in the struggles between the two factions, starting from those arosen inside the Guelph party divided into Whites and Blacks, during the war against Pistoia, in the second half of 1305. Three years of peace and again a war against Volterra, the longest and also the last one for reasons of borderings, of corn fields, of vineyards, for a mistaken sense of honour. At the beginning there were insulting words and skirmishes, then battles. Armed peaces and actual fights last from 1308 to 1324, emptied the treasury and embittered the hearts. At last the mediation of Florence, the real arbitor of Tuscany, was accepted and

the force prevailed as Florence declared that the peace had to be sig
ed otherwise the party that refused the agreement will be punis
ed. During the war against Volterra there was also time to fig
against Henry VII, the German Emperor who gave rise to many
sions for Italians and Dante himself. On Feb. 23, 1313 from Pog
bonsi Henry ordered San Gimignano to pay him 500 pieces of go
and to destroy walls and towers. For a town like San Gimigna
the destruction of walls would have been to take off clothes in t
dephts of winter. San Gimignano repelled this order and luck
Henry died in the 24th August at Buonconvento not far from Sie

The war with Volterra was just finished that another one agair
Lucca started. Master of Lucca was a famous fierce condottie
Castruccio Castracani. At Lucca the merchants of San Gimigna
had many trades, mainly that of saffron. Castruccio protected
Ghibellines driven out of San Gimignano for quarrels with t
Guelph Podestà Ranieri Manteneschi and the Captain of the Pe
ple Gentile Buondelmonti. At the foot of the stairs of the new Po
stà Palace in 1322 some capital executions took place and C
struccio Castracani imposed San Gimignano to take back tho
who had been sent out.

San Gimignano refused and a war burst. The town was involv
in the hostilities that Castruccio had declared against the wh
Guelph league. On the 23rd of September 1325 at Altopascio S
Gimignano's army suffered a terrible defeat and the fire which v
so far away reached the town itself. One of San Gimignano castl
that of Ciuciano, was occupied by the Ghibellines; conquer
again by the Guelphs, it was completely destroyed. A conspira
headed by the Ghibelline Bottaccio Ardinghelli was discovered,
was banished and his houses destroyed. Very close both in ti
and causes were also the fights against Castruccio who had obta
ed from Ludovic the Bavarian the title of Duke of Lucca and had
cluded in his dukedom also San Gimignano. As usual, nobo
gave importance to orders without hearing the interested party. M
over, since the town of Pisa had been included in the Dukedo
San Gimignano recalled from Pisa all the merchants and fou
fiercely against Pisa that had meanwhile reached the walls of S
Gimignano. The unexpected death of Castruccio put an end
these facts that could have taken a bad way.

On the 29th of July 1329 peace was established with Pisa bec
se of tiredness more than conviction, but this peace last only a
years.

In 1332 John of Bohemia, son of Henry VII, came to Italy and
Ghibellines looked up again longing for revenge. They installe
kind of headquarters at the castle of Camporbiano, but on the 1
of September 1332 the soldiers of San Gimignano, led by their
destà and the Captain Piero di Duccio Saracini, assaulted a
burnt the castle. It was a deed of independence and Florence v
not at all satisfied with it. Therefore Florence passed a severe s
tence that luckily was never completely applied. The following y
there was another war against John of Bohemia who wanted
conquer Lucca. Florence was alarmed and asked the help of S
Gimignano in a way that showed the interference of Florence in
interior affairs of San Gimignano.

A few important variations were made on the Statute. Flore
nes took upon themselves the right to own in San Gimignano h
ses and palaces, a right which previously was denied to any stra
ger. It was a mode of putting the hands on the town. Florence t
part in a war against Poggibonsi in 1333. Among the persons v
intervened to establish peace we remind the famous Florentine
orian Giovanni Villani. On the same year all the citizens were c
ed to express their opinion on the municipal road network. Pec
and property of San Gimignano were involved in a war of Flore
against Lucca as well as against Siena that made war to the s
thern castles of its territory. In the years thirties and forties u
1348 the Ardinghellis, come back to San Gimignano in 1331 on

THE CISTERN · On the background view of Tortoli Palace

MARKET PLACE

26

order of Florence, caused riots. Banished again in 1337, when the Duke of Athens in 1342 became Lord of Florence, the Ardinghellis sold him San Gimignano before possessing it and tried to come back to the town as masters. Actually they tried to enter San Gimignano through Porta San Matteo; since this plan failed, they plotted with the Castle of Camporbiano, supported by Florence. The Ardinghellis anyway did not respect some clauses of a treaty and Florence abandoned them.

Nevertheless the Ardinghellis tried by themselves relying on the treason of some friends of theirs who lived in San Gimignano. They failed again and Florence sentenced them to death. They succeeded in persuading Florence to cancel the sentence and were safe. In 1348 a terrible plague killed a great number of persons among whom the sweet Laura loved by Petrarch.

The year of the plague showed new historical developments. The city, even if slowly, was going towards a larger and more open politics. The period of closed Castles was near to finish. The economy restricted on a Communal basis, was trying to reach regional dimensions. San Gimignano was looking for Florence. The General Council decreed to submit to Florence and the deed was signed on the 28th of February 1349. People were afraid to lose their autonomy and so happened on the 11 August 1353. The General Council of Florence consented to the submission of San Gimignano by a majority of one vote. Berardo Ardinghelli signed for San Gimignano and the Podestà Giannotto Camponeschi for Florence. The majority of one vote proved how much puzzled was Florence to rule over a proud and bold town.

PANORAMA

From 1353 to 1530 San Gimignano was under the Florentine ru
One of the most important events during that domination was t
building of «Rocca di Montestaffoli», erected on a pre-existing co
vent of Dominican friars. Today only a few remains are left of th
fortress. During these twohundred years the political activity
San Gimignano marked time. There were just struggles and figh
The town was obliged to pay heavy taxes to Florence for the w
against Bernabò Visconti and Giovanni Acuto and all the expens
for a summit at San Gimignano among Pisa, Lucca, Siena, Arez
Pistoia, Volterra and Florence. Other taxes were paid to fortify t
Castle of Staggia Senese.

Forty years later, in 1411, there was a new plague. In 1431 t
soldiery of Niccolò Piccinino made any kind of browbeatings a
thefts. In 1450 Alphonso of Aragon invaded Florence causi
mournings and ruins. Sigismond Malatesta, the haughtly lord of Ri
ini, came to help Florence and San Gimignano, but his troops ca
sed other ruins. In 1464 a new plague and new scare for the reb
lion of Volterra against Lorenzo the Magnificent.

The historians well disposed for the Medici covered this eve
excusing Volterra and justifying Lorenzo. Some consequenc
poured upon San Gimignano where many heads fell for suspect
connivance with Volterra and Siena.

In 1478 Giuliano dei Medici, brother of Lorenzo, was killed at F
rence in the Church of S. Maria del Fiore as a result of the conspi
cy of Pazzis. San Gimignano took sides with the legitimate pov
and sent a committee of citizens to express solidarity to Medic
family.

The conspiracy was part of a deceitful plan of war against F
rence, organized by Pope Sixtus IV, by king Alphonso of Arag
and by Siena. The enemy army had occupied Poggibonsi, Colle a
Certaldo. The castles of Castellina del Chianti and San Gimigna
repelled the assaults of the Aragonese; San Gimignano was stru
again by the plague that caused five thousand dead. In 1507 Nic
lò Machiavelli came to San Gimignano to organize defence or
more effective basis. The Florentine Republic fell in 1530 and t
Seigniory of Medici was restored. It ruled over Florence and San
mignano until 1737 when the last offspring of Medici, Gian Gas
ne, died. During this period the history of San Gimignano ming
with that of other Tuscan towns. When the era of gunpowder sta
ed, walls and towers lost their political and military importan
Trade branched out on other roads and the Via Francigena was r
along only by farm carts that carried wine, oil, wheat to the la
storehouses of wealthy citizens who lived on private income. Ot
events occurred during the French Revolution and Napoleon's
vasion, but they are not worthy of mention. The former gover
ment of Pietro Leopoldo who was broad-minded about Tusca
had not taken San Gimignano into account. In 1782 Pope Pius
separated the town from the diocesis of Volterra and annexed i
the diocesis of Colle Val d'Elsa. The successors of Leopoldo
not care of San Gimignano and the great travellers of the ni
teenth century, forerunners of modern tourists, did not know S
Gimignano. The town had a period of rest but the instinct of su
val did not die. Nobody had recourse to the pickax to «moderni
the town and when the time of easier communications arrive
young beautiful colourful San Gimignano showed itself from
hills. From the beginning of this century numberless visitors ca
from every part of the world to visit it.

Today you are here, dear visitor, but do not expect to be welcc
ed with the trader's smile on the lips of the people. Beauty, art,
story are not on sale, not even sun, sky, wind and rain which p
among the towers a song never composed.

Enjoy all this as long as you want: San Gimignano will never
exhausted in the coming centuries.

PANORAMA

COUNTRY HOUSE

LANE AND HOUSE OF ST.

ST. FINA

The name of St. Fina is a real symbol of this town. Her slender figure as painted by Ghirlandaio was a miracle of pain and love.

She lived modest and silent and died when she was only fifteen. The vivid gold of her blond hair is found in the violets that every year in March bloom on the black of the towers. Poetical legends of love and sanctity interweave with the few years of her life. The broken amphor that became intact by a sign of cross of her hands; the fruit innocently accepted from a young man enchanted by her beauty; the devil put to flight; the fire of houses extinguished; the angels ringing the bells to announce her death; the violets blooming on the towers on the anniversary of her death (these violets cannot be found elsewhere) and other miracles told by the altar boy of the fresco by Ghirlandaio are concords of grace and poetry.

The Saint lived from 1238 to 1253 and died on an oak board in spirit of penance.

PANORAMA

THE WALL

In consideration of how they were erected and how they are
served, the walls are a living part of San Gimignano. They are
an addition. Without walls the town would not have been
would not be San Gimignano. Castles, palaces, churches, tov
were planned for men; the walls for the town in a sense that is
only topographic. They show the contradiction of mediaeval m
both reserved and hospitable, bold and fearful. Fearful of enem
of strangers, of night-time, of treasons. The walls protected
town giving the sense of the community, of common interests
ideals never denied, not even during the fratricidal wars. W
mean unity and independence, protection of local glory and tr
tion in which every man hands down himself as a person and
people. A document dated 30 December 1214 concerning the
cond ring of walls bears the title «instrumentum franchezze» (s

32

ty deed) and is a definition of the walls as defence of safety and freedom.

The two original cores of San Gimignano were Monte della Torre and Montestaffoli. Surely they were protected with walls, but the first ring enclosing the castle is that starting 1) from Porta dei Becci and dei Cugnanesi, 2) from the Arch of the Cancelleria, 3) from Porta S. Stefano in Canova (near the Prison), 4) from the «postierla» (secret gate in the walls of a town) of Montestaffoli (no more existent). The historian Luigi Pecori, Canon of the Church in the last century, noted that the gates did not show signs of frames or embrasured shutters and added emphatically: «A valid defence were the chest of the citizens». The perimeter of the first enclosure is 1108 metres, the second ring enclosing the present town was finished at the end of 1100 or the beginning of 1200 (the «instrumentum franchezze» is dated 1214) and safety was assured to those who built their houses inside the castle. In 1252 because of the riots, the second enclosure was badly damaged mainly near the gates of St. Matthew and St. John. Ten years later gates and wall were restored. Other smaller gates of this ring are those of Quercecchio, S. Jacopo al Tempio, Bagnaia, Docciola or Mucchiese, Pisana and Corbisso. At the beginning of 1500's five cylindrical towers were added to the western side of the wall. The second enclosure is 2176 metres long.

VIEW OF THE TOWERS

THE TOWER

Once upon a time it was said that San Gimigna
had 72 beautiful towers. Only 25 were standing up
1580. Today they are 14; many others are cut of or a
part of buildings. Their architecture is a sign of su
ty, offense and pride. The first tower (call
Rognosa), 51 metres high, was that of the Podes
and served as office, law court and prison.

Later on were built the tower of the Commune, or Big Tower, at side o the new Palace of the Podestà, embellished, as we can see, with many coats of arms, which remind the various Podestas who contributed to erect it. It is 54 m. high. Then noble families started to built their own towers. They were real fortress-houses with a minimum of comfort. Solid, fire-proof, impenetrable to invasion, light and comfort were sacrificed to safety. The holes visible on the facade were used to throw flying wood bridges to join other friendly families or to attack enemy families. The statute of 1255 prohibited the construction of towers higher than the «Rognosa». It seems that the first family to infringe this order was that of Salvucci who did not build a tower higher than that of the Commune, but two whose height summed up was far superior to that of the public power's tower. The same made the Ghibelline family of Ardinghelli, enemy of Salvuccis. These two couples of towers are at left and right side of the Cathedral square and are called «twin towers».

«At San Gimignano civic buildings offer a great variety of types, a set of samples of structural and decorative motifs pertaining to the Tuscan architecture of the thirteenth and fourteenth conturies: there are Sienese mullioned windows, Florentine windows, Pisan arches and majolica plates, Lucchese and Sienese brick arched lintels, pointed arcade crownings surmounted by battlements and juting out penthouses. There is also some oriental sign coming from Pisa, with which San Gimignano had strong commercial links, or directly from the East where Sangimignanese traders, alone or in connection with those of Pisa and Florence, had shops for the sale of saffron, honey and other wares. Rightly it was said that San Gimignano is a museum of mediaeval Tuscan houses.» (San Gimignano, Historical Hints by Giovanni Cecchini - Artistic notes by Enzo Carli, Siena, 1962).

TOURIS

ITINERARIES

For those who have time and desire to stay a few days at San Gimignano, the town has been divided into three itineraries to be gone along without haste: haste does not get along with art. Those who have a shorter time at their disposal, can visit the town in a few hours, not forgetting, however, to stop in Cathedral square.

CATHEDRAL · Towards the Calvary · (Detail)
(Barna from Siena, 1380)

CATHEDRAL SQUARE and TOWN HALL

Let's visit the town starting from Cathedral Square as far as the various itineraries are concerned (they can be walked along in a few hours).

Going up the stairs leading to the Church, if we turn our back to the Cathedral, in front of us, on a deep vault, we see the Tower of the Podestà (called Rognosa, 51 metres high). It dates back to 1200 and dominates the ancient Podestà Palace. At its side the elegant 1208's Chigi Mansion (formerly Useppi) with tower and adjacent to it a mediaeval house with mullioned windows. On the right side dominates the 54 m. high Town Tower called Big Tower as it is higher than all the others. Started on the 21 August 1300 (four months after the visit of Dante) it was finished in 1311. At the side of the Town Hall (deserving a visit) there is the People Loggia finished in 1347 on the ground of Ardinghelli family who had their house pulled down after their attempt to take possession of the power over the town.

39

The memorial tablet on the facade between the two doors, reminds Pope Eugene III who on the 21 November 1148 consecrate this temple. The Church was substituting and incorporating a pexiting oratory dating back to the 9th or 10th century, the traces which are visible along the interior walls of the facade. Of the basilica-planned church we do not know the name of the first builders, but the raising of the central nave is ascribed to the Lomba master Brunisemd and to the Sangimignanese Gamo Gamuc The church underwent some adjustments, the most important o being that made in 1466 by the Florentine Giuliano da Maiano whtransformed the presbyteral part by extending the choir and addisix chapels to the transept, three on each side. Giuliano da Maia

CATHEDRAL · Angel and Madonna (Jacopo della Quercia)

is also the author of the Chapel which keeps the remains of St. Fina. In the same period in front of St. Fina's was interrupted a wing of the Cloister leading to the cemetery.

Interior wall of the facade:
- remains of the apse of the pre-existing church.
- Our Lady of the Annunciation and Announcing Angel, two wooden statues by Jacopo della Quercia (1421), polychromed by Martino di Bartolomeo in 1426, as it is stated by an inscription on the base of the Virgin's statue. The classical plastic art of the Archangel Gabriel emphasizes the softness of the Madonna's face and figure. The two statues among the many wooden ones are certainly ascribable to the Sienese sculptor. On the accounting books of the Collegiate Church they are mentioned as «by Maestro Jacopo of the Fount of Siena».

CATHEDRAL · St. Sebastian (Benozzo Gozzoli, 1465)

- St. Sebastian's martyrdom by Benozzo Gozzoli (1465); G
  briele d'Annunzio liked this fresco very much. On the p
  lars: St. Augustine, St. Bernard, St. Jerome, and St. B
  nardine.

On the upper part:

- Last judgement by Taddeo di Bartolo (1393), with scen
  of such a realism that becomes grotesque.

Left wall, entering the church:

- episodes of the Old Testament, from Genesis to the Bo
  of Job by the Sienese artist Bartolo di Fredi (1367). T
  paintings were retouched during the eighteenth centu
  but tests have alrealdy been made to bring them back
  their original colours. Through the freshness of his art t
  painter has expressed biblical events lit up with folk-l
  poetry, a sign of the easiness and immediacy of his a
  He was not worried by the important themes his bru
  was dealing with. He reproduced faces, dresses, manne
  of his time daily life to represent events and situatio
  that reflect the history of man in all the epochs (see t
  main facts of Job's life).

Main altar:

- Ciborium and adoring Angels by Benedetto da Maiano (
  cond half of the fifteenth century).

CATHEDRAL · Hell: Sloth (Taddeo di Bartolo, 1396)

44

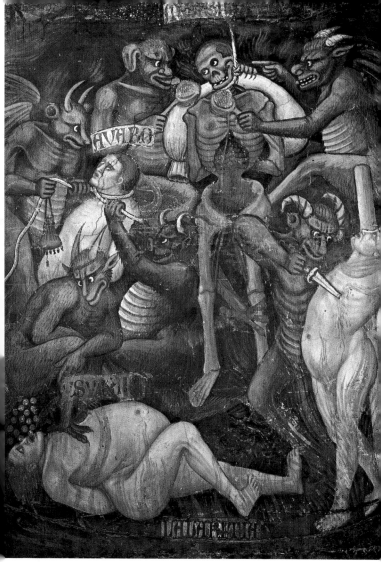

CATHEDRAL
Hell: Avarice
(Taddeo di Bartolo, 1396)

Right wall:
  • Life of Christ by Barna da Siena (towards the half of the
    fourteenth century) «one of the most conspicuous mo-
    ments of the Sienese painting in the fourteenth century»
    (Enzo Carli). Barna died while painting the crucifixion sce-
    ne. He fell down from the scaffolding he was working on,
    while stepping back to look at his painting. Vasari wrote:
    «He fell down from the scaffolding in such a strange way
    that he was crushed inside and so indecently broken that
    two days later he passed away from this life». A pupil of
    Barna finished the work. His name was Giovanni d'Ascia-
    no. The scene of the crucifixion was damaged by war
    events on July 1944. The painting is strongly and highly

CATHEDRAL
Hell: Gluttony
(Taddeo di Bartolo, 1396)

46

CATHEDRAL
Hell: Adultery
(Taddeo di Bartolo, 1396)

47

CATHEDRAL - Crossing of the Red Sea (Bartolo di Fredi, 1356)

CATHEDRAL - Moses on Mount Sinai - Temptation of Job
(Bartolo di Fredi, 1356)

dramatic. Note the scene of Judah's kiss, of Christ going up to Calvary, above all the Crucifixion. The painting of Barna is vigorous and his brush although that of a Sienese, does not get lost in the preciousness of colours. The artist and the onlooker take part in the scene and this participation is originated by the penetration into the bottom of the figures more than by the lecture of the events. It has been said that the results attained by the artist are those of a «sacred representation».

Beside the Crucifixion:

- Chapel of St. Fina, designed by Giuliano da Maiano, was begun in 1468 and finished in 1475. The beautiful altar is by Benedetto da Maiano, one of Giuliano's brothers. A great artist, A. Rossellino, gave some hints to carry out the chapel. The wall paintings are by Domenico Ghirlandaio and represent two events of St. Fina's life: Pope Gregory appears to the Saint and the obsequies for her death. Sebastiano Mainardi, a Sangimignanese painter and a relative of Ghirlandaio, painted the frescoes of the vault (1477). The Cahpel was consecrated in 1488 by Niccolò, Bishop of Pistoia. Four artists among the most famous of the Florentine fifteenth century, made of this room a real jewel. Three of them were Giuliano and Benedetto da Maiano and Domenico Ghirlandaio.

Friar Giovanni del Coppo, the first biographer of the Saint,

CATHEDRAL · The devil Killing Job's herd and army
Job's sons buried under the houses (Bartolo di Fredi, 1356)

CATHEDRAL · Jesus walks on the water (Barna da Siena, 1380

CATHEDRAL · Judas sells Christ (Barna da Siena, 1380)

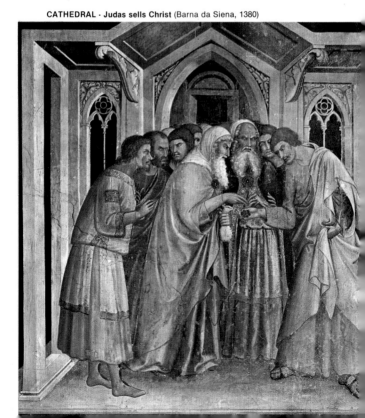

CATHEDRAL
Christ crowned with thorns
(Barna da Siena, 1380)

51

CATHEDRAL
Jesus bearing the Cross
(Barna da Siena, 1380

CATHEDRAL
Baptism of Christ
(Barna da Siena, 1380)

CATEDRAL · Resurrection of Lazarus (Barna da Siena, 1380)

CATHEDRAL · Christ at the Praetorium (Barna da Siena, 1380)

CATHEDRAL · Christ among the doctors (Barna da Siena, 1380)

CATHEDRAL · Christ praying in the olive garden (Barna da Siena, 1380)

CATHEDRAL
Transfiguration
(Barna da Siena, 1380)

CATHEDRAL
Crucifixion
(Barna da Siena, 1380)

CATHEDRAL · St. Fina's Chapel: St. Gregory appears to St. Fina
(Domenico Ghirlandaio)

CATHEDRAL · St. Fina's Chapel: Obsequi
(Domenico Ghirlandaio)

TABERNACLE OF SANTA FINA

buried here, related that Fina's parents, Cambio and Impe-
ria, chose that name for their little daughter because the
mother, while expecting the baby had a feeling that she
was about to give life to a particularly precious being «de-
licate, fine» and so Fina had this name. Visiting the chapel
one receives the impression of such finesse. Looking up
from the entrance, on a lunette of the nave arch, we see a
fresco of the first half of the fourteenth century ascribed
to Niccolò di Segna representing St. Gregory appearing to
St. Fina dying. It is the first iconographical testimony of
the veneration of the Saint.

PECORI SQUARE - St. John's oratory - On the wall in background:
Annunciation (D. Ghirlandaio, 1482)

MUSEUM OF SACRED ART · Crucifix (Unknown author, 1100)

60

ANNUNCIATION (D. Ghirlandaio, 1482)

PECORI SQUARE

Coming out of the Church and going bejond an arch (on the right) having a statue of St. Gimignano formerly on the Porta delle Fonti, we enter the Luigi Pecori Square. Mons. Pecori, Canon of the Basilica in the 19th century, was the best historian of San Gimignano. He wrote the «History of the territory of San Gimignano» published in Florence in 1853. On the right there are the ruins of an arcade which linked the Piazza to the ancient Cemetery at that time located where today is the sacristy. In 1482 below the arches was built a chapel painted by Ghirlandaio with an «Annunciation» on behalf of Giuliano di Martino Cetti. Afterwards, in 1623 the Baptismal Font was moved from the Basilica nearby the «Woman's Gate» (right nave) to the Chapel. The place has been restored recently (1959). The arcades were reopened and the upper loggia restored; it shelters now the Museum of Sacred Art containing precious ancient sacred vessels and vestments.

(To visit the museum apply to the Basilica's sacristan).

ONOPHRIO PETRI TEMPLI
HVIVS REPARATORI
GRATI CIVES POS

MUSEUM OF SACRED ART
(Giuliano from Maiano, 1476)

TOWN HALL,
ALSO CALLED NEW PALACE
OF THE PODESTA'

Going back to the Cathedral Square, at its side we see the Town Hall whose construction commenced in the second half of the 13th century, was finished on the 23 of December 1288. That same day the Town Council gathered for the first time. It is the only authentic Palace of the Podestà. The other, known as «ancient» did not serve for the Council meetings, but it was the Podestà's residence and the jail. Ten years later, in 1311, the Town Hall was flanked by the

COURTYARD OF THE TOWN HALL

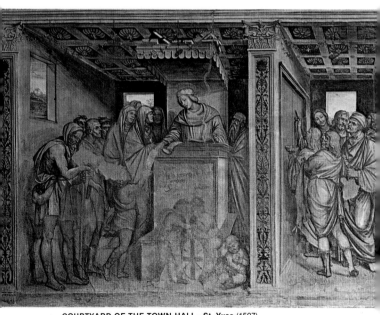

COURTYARD OF THE TOWN HALL · St. Yves (1507)
(Antonio Bazzi called the Sodoma, 1477-1549)

Big Tower. Originally the palace was smaller, but in 1323 the original plan ascribed to the famous architect Arnolfo di Cambio from Colle Val d'Elsa, was enlarged. On the right side we see the Loggia or Tribune from where the Podestà delivered the oath of fidelity to the town. At the foot of its stairs in 1352 Primerano and Rossellino of the Ardinghelli family were beheaded. The heavy battlement was added in 1811.

Going beyond the door reading «Museo Civico» (Town Museum) we come to a courtyard built in 1323 when the palace was enlarged.

The interior walls bears the coats-of-arms of some Podestas. They render living these citizens dead long ago. The cistern was sunk in 1360 when Jacopo di Carroccio Alberti was Podestà. Here and there some Etruscan cinerary urns. On the right there is the Loggia of the Judge. The three wall frescoes are related to the justice that was administred here. The upper fresco represents Our Lady with the Child who bears a scroll reading: «Diligite iustitiam qui iudicatis terram» (Love the justice you who judge on the earth). The Madonna has at her sides St. Gregory and St. Gimignano. On the right a large fresco by Sodoma (1507) represents St. Yves (the French canonist, patron saint of lawyers and a lawyer himself).

A number of citizens throng around his bench. The Saint renders justice to a child while out of his office a group of other citizens who carry presents, are waiting for justice. An unknown character looks after that nobody try to corrupt the judge.

Of the incorruptibility of the justice an unknown citizen of the 16th century was not much convinced if he wrote on the chair: «I promise you win the suit, if you are prompt with the (pouch)».

The third painting is an allegory probably by the same Sodoma (1513). From his chair the judge drives out Lie dragging at his feet; at his right a snake symbolizes Prudence and a naked woman (left) Truth. Above is an inscription:

«Man suffers for his sins:
draw the truth out of lie,
false tongue does always falsify».

Above the exit of the corridor through which we entered, there is a fresco by Cesare Vagarini (a living Sangimignanese painter) representing Prudence, Justice and Fortitude.

MUSEUM

Two flights of stairs and a landing dating back to 1323 lead
the Museum

Dante Hall

The first hall on the second floor is called Dante's Hall for t
reason that Alighieri spoke from here on the 8th of May 1300 ai
ing to rekindle the Guelph ideals. The wall facing the windows
covered with a large fresco by Lippo Memmi of Siena. The fresc
signed and dated 1317, represents Our Lady on the throne and w
ordered by the Sienese Podestà Nello dei Tolomei who is portray
at the feet of the Madonna and stands out among twenty-sev
personages. Because of the richness of gold, the harmonious co
position of colours, the religious elegance of figures, the hiera
solemnity of the assembly, this painting was named «Maestà» (n
jesty) like that by Simone Martini in the Town Hall of Siena. The f
sco was partially retouched by Benozzo Gozzoli in 1416 on the
casion of the opening of the two Renaissance doors, when
Francis and St. Ludovic (right) and St. Anthony (left) were comp
tely repainted. On the back wall and around, hunting scenes a
people paying homage to Charles II of Anjou, painted by Azzo
Siena in 1292. Dante admired these paintings. On the place or
occupied by the Podestà an inscription:
«Judge
Listen to everybody's proposal
answer graciously and do justice» (1).
From Dante's Hall, through the left door, we reach the hall of
cret assemblies or Priors Hall. Note the wooden benches carvec
1473 and a glass urn containing St. Bartholus, a work by Giova
Gonnelli called «the blind man of Gambassi» (16th century).
From this hall we go to that where precious terracotta pots or
in the pharmacy of St. Fina are kept.

(1) Until a few years ago a Town Hall policeman who volunteered kind
guide visitors just for his town's sake, amused himself reading as foll
«Judge, listen to everybody's proposal, answer graciously and do as
like». If somebody asked him why he read the inscription (which can be
dly deciphered) in that way, he candidly answered: «At San Gimignano w
ve always done so».

TOWN MUSEUM · Wedding scenes   (Niccolò di Segna, 12th century)

TOWN MUSEUM · Dante's Hall: Majesty (Lippo Memmi, 1317)

Chapel of the Podestà

Coming out from Dante's Hall and going up a flight of stairs, we
see on the left the Podestà's chapel, dedicated to the Holy Trinity.
Coming in, on the left we see:
- Madonna with Child and figures of Saints, by Domenico
  Mainardi from San Gimignano (second half of the 15th
  century).
- Pietà, a detached fresco ascribed to the school of Benoz-
  zo Gozzoli.
- Crucifix with St. Francis and St. Jerome, detached fresco
  ascribed to the school of Benozzo Gozzoli.
- Our Lady with the Child and the Saints Justus and Tho-
  mas, a work by the painter Pier Francesco called «Floren-
  tine priest», dated 1476.
- The Holy Trinity by the same painter.
- Our Lady with the Child, St. Bartholomew and St. Anthony
  by Pier Francesco (1490).

Picture Gallery

First Room
Coming in, from the right side:
- Crucifix with Passion's facts by the Florentine Coppo di Marcovaldo. The execution of the work takes us back to Montaperti battle (September 1260) in which the painter took part. Being prisoner of the Sienese, for his liberation he painted the famous Madonna in the Basilica dei Servi at Siena, and this Crucifix. «The tragically vehement inspiration of this painter contemporary with Cimabue is revealed by the vigorous drawing and by the strong contrast between light and shade creating effects of intense plasticity» (E. Carli).
- Madonna with the Child, St. Gregory, St. John Baptist, St. Francis, St. Fina, by Domenico Michelino, a Florentine painter who lived from 1417 to 1491.
- Madonna with the Child, St. John Baptist, St. Mary Magdalen, St. Augustine, St. Martha, by Benozzo Gozzoli. The work is dated 1466 and signed.
- Madonna with the Child, St. Jerome and St. Bernard. Over the altar step, nativity of the Virgin by Bartolomeo di Giovanni (1502).
- Madonna with the Child, St. Andrew and St. Prosperus, over the altar step: Pietà by Benozzo Gozzoli (1466).
- Madonna with the Child, St. John and an Angel, by Sebastiano Mainardi, beginning of the 16th century.
- Our Lady of the Annunciation and an announcing Angel, two tondi by Filippino Lippi. This work was ordered to the painter (son of Filippo Lippi and pupil of Botticelli) on the 9 January 1482.
- Madonna in glory, St. Gregory and St. Benedict by Bernardo di Betto called Pinturicchio (1512). He had this nickname because of his poor physical constitution («un pinturicchio, sordicchio e brutticchio» = a little painter, a little deaf and a little ugly). The picture was painted for the Monastery of Monteoliveto Minore (a beautiful complex nearby San Gimignano, deserving a visit).
- Madonna with the Child and two adoring Angels, by Bartolomeo di Giovanni, end of the 15th century.
- Madonna with the Child, St. Nicholas of Tolentino, St. Michael Archangel, St. Augustine, St. Lucy, by Vincenzo Tamagni of San Gimignano (first half of the 16th century).
- Pietà and events of the passion, school of Neri di Bicci, 15th century.
- Madonna with the Child by Neri di Bicci.
- Crucifixion with figures, by an unknown painter from Siena, 13th century.

TOWN MUSEUM
Crucifixion
(Unknown Sienese painter, 1285-1295)

/N MUSEUM · Madonna with the Child
ozzo Gozzoli, 1420-1497)

TOWN MUSEUM · Madonna with the Child
At her sides: St. John Baptist, St. Mary Magdalen,
(Benozzo Gozzoli, 1466)

TOWN MUSEUM
Announcing Angel
(Filippino Lippi, 1482)

TOWN MUSEUM
Our Lady of Annunciation
(Filippino Lippi, 1482)

TOWN MUSEUM
Madonna in glory
(Pinturicchio)

74

Second Room
- St Julian, St. Antony Abbot, St. Martin, by an unknown Florentine painter (1419).
- St. Bartholomew and events of his life (1401) by Lorenzo di Niccolò Gerini.
- Events of St. Fina by the same author. They are painted on the doors of the urn which kept the relics of the Saint before the building of her chapel in the Cathedral. It is a nice work and shows the most famous events in the life of the Saint of the violets, of whom it is a valid iconographic gallery. Front side: Pope Gregory the Great, St. Fina with violets and the town in her hands. Right door, above: St. Fina ill is nursed by her mother while a relative tries to drive out the rats infesting her couch. Below: the devil flings St. Fina's mother out of the stairs, but she is unharmed. On the left door: procession to the corpse of St. Fina laid out on an oak bed bloomed miraculously with yellow violets. Below: funeral of the Saint and cure of the paralysed hand of her nurse Beldia. On the back: four miracles of the Saint.
- recovery of a possessed person (the devil comes out of his mouth).
- rescue of a brick-layer fallen from the roof.
- rescue of a shipwrecked man.
- putting out of a fire in the town by a dress of the Saint.
- Our Lady of the Annunciation by an unknown author (beginning of the 15th century).
- Madonna with the Child by Lorenzo di Niccolò Gerini.
- Sacred image by the Florentine painter Pseudo Ambrogio di Baldese (beginning of the 15th century).
- Sacred image by an unknown Florentine painter (15th century).
- Sacred image by an unknown Sienese painter (15th century).

Third Room (from the right):
- Cross painted and shaped by un unknown Florentine artist (first half of the 15th century).
- Madonna with the Child and figures of Saints by Guido da Siena. The painting was carried to San Gimignano in 1280 when the Convent of St. Augustine was built.
- Female heads, fragment of a fresco by Bartolo di Fredi (half of the 14th century).
- Madonna with the Child by Vincenzo Tamagni.
- Madonna with the Child by an unknown Sienese painter (13th century).
- The Bishop of San Gimignano and events of his life, by Taddeo di Bartolo (1363-1422).
- Chest for keeping the wedding dowry.
- Assumption with St. John Evangelist, St. Bernard, St. Catherine of Alexandria, St. Bartholomew, by Niccolò Tagliacci, a painter from Siena (first half of the 14th century).
- Madonna with the Child, St. Peter, St. John Evangelist, St. Michael, St. Francis, St. Chiara, by an unknown author.
- Crucifixion and various figures, by an unknown Sienese painter (end of the 13th century).

TOWN MUSEUM
Crucifix by Coppo of Marcovaldo

Room of the Podestà

Coming out from the art gallery, on the stair landing is the Room of the Podestà. Built at the beginning of the 14th century, it was frescoed with erotic scenes by the painter Azzo.

Those who like it, can go up to the Big Tower to admire the most beautiful panorama of the Tuscan countryside.

FORTRESS OF MONTESTAFFOLI

Coming out of the square, turn to the right corner of the Cathedral and get into the Piazza delle Erbe (Erbe means vegetables and it was so called because here was the market place). From here we go up to the Fortress situated on the highest spot of the town. It was built in 1353, when San Gimignano devoted itself to Florence, on a pre-existing Dominican Convent. The fortress lost every military importance in 1555 when Cosimo I ordered its destruction.

From one of the towers we can enjoy one of the most characteristic views of the towers as well as of the Valdelsa countryside.

FORTRESS OF MONTESTAFFOLI

St. MATTHEW STREET

SECOND ITINERARY
☐ Cathedral Square
☐ Via San Matteo
☐ Piazza S. Agostino

From the Cathedral Square, going beyond the Arch of the Chancery, we get into Via S. Matteo. This street is flanked with palaces dating back to the 12th and 13th centuries with nice mullioned windows. Note at the beginning, the Palace of the Chancery (14th century), the Tower-House of Nomi Pesciolini (also called Palace of King Desiderius); the Church of St. Bartholus; in front, a Moresque-styled house; on the right, at number 60, the Tinacci Palace with three lines of windows. Going on to the Gate (Porta S. Matteo, of which one enjoys a comprehensive view from out of the walls), through Vicolo Cellolese, we turn to left and reach Piazza S. Agostino.

Church of St. Augustine

On the square paved in herring-bone shape (12th century Romanesque style) there are the Church of St. Peter and the Church of St. Augustine. The Church of St. Peter belongs to the Bishop's See of Volterra, reminding the mastery of this town over San Gimignano. To visit it, apply to the Augustinian Friars. Inside, there are some interesting paintings of the Sienese school, perhaps by Barna himself.

The Church of St. Augustine, together with the Convent, was built from 1280 to 1298. Its style is Gothic, even if Gothic constructive elements are not applied to a great extent. It has only one nave with a rectangular apse, flanked by smaller chapels. During a recent restoration the ogival windows were brought to light.

First of all pay a visit to the choir's paintings behind the main altar. Benozzo Gozzoli painted on the walls the life of St. Augustine, one of the greatest thinkers of the Christianity. At first sight one draws the impression of freshness, of visual taste, of pleasant reading. The Florentine painter gave here the best of his art and of his skill in a harmonious composition of colours which gratifies the eyes and expresses with some biographical fidelity the life of the saint.

The whole work was made from 1463 to 1465.

Starting from left the paintings represent:
- the parents of Augustine entrust their child to the teacher of Tagaste.
- Augustine enters the Unuversity of Carthago.
- Augustine travelling for Italy.
- The landing at Ostia.
- Augustine teaches in Rome.
- Augustine leaves for Milan.
- Augustine meets in Milan the Bishop Ambrose and the Emperor Theodosius.
- Augustine listens to a homily of St. Ambrose; his mother Monica implores St. Ambrose for the conversion of her son; disputation of Augustine with St. Ambrose.
- Augustine meditates over the letters of St. Paul.
- Augustine is baptized.
- Augustine visits the Convent of Monte Pisano; an angel appearing as a child, tries to pour off the sea water into a puddle thus dissuading Augustine to inquire about the mystery of the Holy Trinity relying only on the reason.
- Death of St. Monica; above, left, St. Augustine talks to his mother; below, right, St. Augustine goes back to Africa.
- Augustine blesses people after being consecrated Bishop of Hippon.
- Augustine debates victoriously with the heretic Manichean Fortunatus once his school-mate.
- Augustine in ecstasy talks to St. Jerome.
- Exequies of the Saint.
  In the vault the four Evangelists; on the pillars figures of saints.

ST. AUGUSTINE'S CHURCH · Facade

ST. AUGUSTINE'S CHURCH · Interior

ST. AUGUSTINE'S CHURCH · St. Augustine discussing with the infant Jesus about the mystery of Trinity (Benozzo Gozzoli, 1465)

ST. AUGUSTINE'S CHURCH · Coronation of Mary
(Piero del Pollaiolo, 1483)

- On the main altar a large painting by the Florentine p[ain]
  ter Piero Pollaiolo brother of the greater Antonio. [The]
  painting represents the conoration of the Virgin Mary. [Be]
  low, left, St. Fina, St. Augustine, St. Bartholus Bompe[g]
  ni, St. Gimignano, St. Jerome (beating his breast wit[h a]
  stone) and St. Nicholas of Tolentino. Below the date of [the]
  painting: 1483. This work was ordered by Domen[ico]
  Strambi, Prior of the Convent. At first sight the pain[ting]
  strikes because of its monotony of colours (but it is ju[st]
  deterioration caused by time) and its static composit[ion].
  Nevertheless it is one of the most considerable work[s of]
  the Florentine fifteenth century (see the face of St. [Bar]
  tholus, below).

82

- In the right chapel, looking at the main altar: frescoes by Bartolo di Fredi (1356) with Birth and Assumption of the Virgin. On the altar: a work by Vincenzo Tamagni (1523) ordered to the painter by Ippolita Saracini who wanted to be portraited on her knees.
- Coming down from the Presbytery, on the left, we see a painting by Giovanni Balducci (Andrea del Sarto's School): mystic marriage of St. Catherine of Siena.
- Past the side door, the Tinacci's altar with a painting by Pier Francesco, called Florentine priest, representing Our Lady with the Child and Saints (1494). Above, the Pietà, a fresco by Vincenzo Tamagni.
- At the end of the Church is the Chapel of St. Bartholus. The Saint was so much patient that was called «Job of Tuscany». The Chapel was built in 1448 at the expense of the Commune and of the Hospital of St. Fina. It was Benedetto da Maiano who planned and built it (second half of the 15th century). Under the artist's hand the marble seems to lose its materiality and from the sculptures of the monument emanates an aura of serenity and composure that gives the impression of holiness winning over death and eternity winning over time. The lower part reminds a few episodes of the saint priest's life. On the sarcophagus, the statues of Faith, Hope and Charity. Above, the wonderful tondo of the Madonna with the Child and two angels. The paintings on the right are by Sebastiano Mainardi, a painter of San Gimignano, and represent St. Nicholas of Bari, St. Lucy, St. Gimignano.
- Going towards the main Altar, we find a fresco by V. Tamagni representing the adoration of the Cross. The Crucifix is missing. On the same wall is a fresco by Benozzo Gozzoli representing St. Sebastiano. It was ordered to the painter for the plague of 1464. The Saint's intercession stopped the darts of the Lord's chastisement and protected people at his feet. Our eyes do not get tired of admiring one by one the faces of common people, expecially children, figures idealized in their realistic appearance: in other words a moment and a document of life presented by art in the complete autonomy of its free means.
- The marble bust represents Niccolò Pesciolini, a valiant soldier dead in 1619.
- The pulpit with Posca family's coat of arms dates back to 1524; the paintings surrounding it, are by V. Tamagni.
- The fresco of Our lady over the baroque altar is by Lippo Memmi who painted it in 1330. Unfortunately the work has lost all interest as a consequence of bad restoration. Both the Madonna and the Archangel St. Michael are cold adjustments of the ancient figures.
- Closer to the Presbytery there is an interesting fresco. It was made by Sebastiano Mainardi (1488) and represents St. Gimignano, Bishop of Modena, surrounded by Mattia Lupi, a poet, Domenico Mainardi, a canonist, and Nello Nelli dei Cetti, a jurisconsult; below, the corpse of Fra Domenico Strambi, the great Sangimignanese scholar called «Parisian doctor» who taught philosophy at the Sorbonne in Paris. It was he who asked Benozzo Gozzoli to come to San Gimignano.
- In the chapel, close to the main altar, there are two paintings, one by Giovanni Balducci (1589) which is the last important work made in San Gimignano after the city's decadence, and the other by Fra Paolino of Pistoia (1490-1547) rich in not so well amalgamate colours. Balducci represented the Madonna slipping a ring on to a finger of St. Catherine of Alexandria. Friar Paolino painted the Madonna with the Child and the Saints Nicholas of Bari, Catherine and Vincent Ferreri.

- Entering the sacristy we reach the Cloister of the Conve
  having two lines of arcades full of peace and light.

  Once come back to the square, we reach Via 20 Settem
  and from here the Hospital of St. Fina built in 1255 w
  the offerings collected after her death. Note in the entr
  ce hall two busts representing St. Gregory and St. Fina
  work by Piero Torgianni, the violent tempered sculp
  who deformed the face of Michael Angelo with a fist.
  sculptures are a gift of the learned Sangimignanese pri
  Stefano Coppi and date back to the end of the 15th cen
  ry. Going further along the street we see the 11th cent
  Church of St. James. Inside a 14th century painting of
  Sienese school (Lippo and Memmo Memmi) is notewort
  The church was built by Sangimignanese knights on th
  return from the first Crusade. On the front is a nice te
  cotta rose-window.

  Coming back to the town centre, on Via 20 Settembre,
  fore the Hospital, there is the Church of St. Jerome wh
  keeps a painting by Vincenzo Tamagni representing
  Virgin Mary with Saints. The St. Jerome behind the alta
  by Mainardi. Other interesting paintings are to be foun
  the Conservatory of S. Chiara (in front of the steep Via
  le Fonti): a Madonna with Saints by V. Tamagni is no
  worthy.
- From Via delle Fonti we go down to the buildings of
  same name (13th and 14th centuries) with Romanesc
  and Gothic arches. It is a part of ancient San Gimigna
  luckily kept intact.

ST. AGUSTINE'S CHURCH · Altar of St. Bartholus
(Benedetto da Maiano)

COISTER OF ST. AUGUSTINE

THE FOUNTAINS

CISTERN SQUARE

CISTERN SQUARE

From the Cathedral Square, beyond the People Loggia we reach the Cistern Square. Once here was the trade and bank centre. The square derives its name from an artistic travertine cistern dating back to 1237. Its real name is Caves Square or Elm Square (because of an elm tree once existing at a side of the square near the passage leading to Porta dei Cugnanesi. In middle ages the elm was a symbol of fidelity).

- The square is delimited by interesting palaces and towers among which the «twin towers» belonging to Ardinghellis. A little farther there is the Devil's tower: a legend tells that its owner, when back from a trip, found it higher than when he had left and believed that such elevation had been made by the devil. At foot of the tower is Vicolo dell'Oro (Gold Lane) so called because once gold-beaters had here their shops.
- At the centre of the square there is the Cistern with the coat of arms of the Podestà Guccio Malvolti who had it enlarged in 1346. People think that the visitor who turns around the cistern sooner or later will come back to San Gimignano. Going on towards Via del Castello (in front of the Cistern) we find at its end the Church of St. Lawrence dating back to the 13th century. Inside there are interesting paintings which represent the various cycles of transmundane worlds.The Paradise and Christ with the twelve Apostles are well preserved. All around some ancient frescoes irreparably lost.
- Close to the Church, in the Oratory, is a wonderful Madonna surrounded by small heads of angels. The work is ascribed to Cenno di Francesco Cenni, a 15th century Florentine painter. The other paintings are also ascribed to him.
- Coming out of the Church, the gloomy big building beyond Via del Castello is the Penitentiary; once it was a Dominican Convent and Girolamo Savonarola was among the friars who lived in.

ST. JOHN STREET with a view of St. Francis' Church

VIA S. GIOVANNI

Back to Piazza della Cisterna, going beyond the ancient Po
dei Cugnanesi, we reach Via S. Giovanni. Halfway there is the P
tellesi Palace with mullioned windows, once the Monastery of
Catherine and presently the seat of the Town Library. In the inter
note the frescoes by V. Tamagni. Farther on but opposite, there
the Church formerly of St. John, belonged to the Knights Temp
in the 12th century and later to the Knights of Malta. Above t
door there is the characteristic circumscribed Templar Cross.

ST. JOHN GATE

Outside Porta S. Giovanni there is the Remembrance Park w
the War Memorial for the soldiers dead in the 1915-18 war; on
left, looking at the gate, rises the 15th century Round Bulwark wh
Niccolò Machiavelli instructed the soldiers to drill with the ar
«claiming to Italy - reads a tablet on the keep - the right to fight a
to shed blood for the country».

Once back to the town, if you dispose of sufficient time, foll
the stairs on the left of the Gate and go along Via Berignano to c
cover breath-taking views of San Gimignano. From Via Querc
chio, turning to right, return to Via S. Giovanni and through the C
gnanesi Arch, come back to Cistern Square.

ST. JOHN GATE

VIEW OF THE ROMANESQUE CHURCH OF CELLOLE (15th century)

SURROUNDINGS OF SAN GIMIGNANO

Church of Cellole

At about 4 Km from San Gimignano on the Via San Matteo's side there is the ancient Church of Cellole. It was built at the beginning of 1100 and has three naves in carved travertine and offers a sight of coarse mysticism. Its never altered Romanesque style unfold

INSIDE VIEW OF THE CHURCH OF CELLOLE

ST. MATTHEW GA

its vigour. In the apse there is a line of stones engraved with still mysterious symbols. This Church struck the imagination of Giacomo Puccini who drew inspiration for a scene of his «Suor Angelica».

Castle of Castelvecchio

At 5 Km from San Gimignano, coming out from Porta San Giovanni, nearby Cornocchio you can see the ruins of a castle that since 1200 was allied to San Gimignano against Volterra. It slowly decayed since the beginning of the 14th century.

Church of Monteoliveto

At about one kilometre from the side of the War Memorial rises the formerly Convent of Monteoliveto built by the Sangimignanese knight Gualtiero Salvucci. The church keeps now baroque lines. Nearby the three-arched front portico we enjoy one of the most beautiful views of San Gimignano. In the 15th century cloister (recently restored) we can admire.
- a Crucifixion with Our Lady and St. John by Benozzo Gozzoli dating back to 1467.
  A painting by Friar Paolino of Pistoia is kept in the Church of St. Lucy not far from Monteoliveto: it represents a Madonna in throne with saints. On the base of the frame is a Visitation dating back to 1525.
  Frescoes and paintings of some value by the Florentine painter Pier Francesco (15th century) are at Pancole (a celebrated Marian shrine), at St. Lucy's and at Ulignano. At Cusona there is a painting by Bartolo di Fredi representing the Madonna of the Roses; at Casaglia a painting by Andrea del Sarto represents the Holy Family (1500).

ST. JAMES' CHURCH (11th century)

CONTENTS

Tourist Itineraries

WHAT TO EAT

Ravioli with cottage che
rice and soup à la Sangimi
nese, roasts on the spit, Flc
tine chops, wild boars, ha
pheasants, thrushes, sausa
salami, mortadella, she
milk cheese, truffles.
Wines: Vernaccia, Vinsa
Malvasia (Malmsey), Chiant

SCINA

AR

ARCO

ARCHEGGIO
RIVATO

SWIMMING-POOL

BAR

PARK

PRIVATE
PARKING

HOTEL "LE RENAIE"
RISTORANTE "LEONETTO"

CINA TIPICA TOSCANA

TYPICAL TUSCAN CUISINE

Loc. Pancole — 53037 SAN GIMIGNANO (Siena)

TEL: Telefono (0577) 95.50.44

ST. : Telefono (0577) 95.50.72

Telefax (0577) 95.50.44

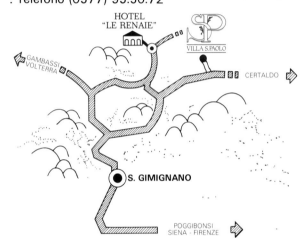

TEL **VILLA S. PAOLO** ★ ★ ★ ★

ada Provinciale CERTALDO — 53037 SAN GIMIGNANO (Siena)
Telefono (0577) 95.51.00 — Telefax (0577) 95.51.00

cina - Parco secolare - Bar - Parcheggio privato
TV color - Frigo bar - Aria condizionata

imming-pool - Secular park - Bar - Private parking
Colour TV - Refrigerator bar - Air conditioning

1 - War Memorial

 2 - St. John's Gate

3 - Pratellesi Palace
    (Town Library)

 4 - Cugnanesi's Arch

5 - Church of S. Lorenzo
    in Ponte

 6 - Tortoli Palace (XV century)

Restaurant

LA GRIGLIA

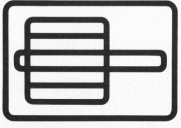

San Gimignano - Historical centre
Via San Matteo, 34/36 - Tel. 0577/940.005

SPECIAL DISHES
WILD BOAR PÂTÉ AND HAM
TRUFFLES AND MUSHROOMS
MIXED GRILL
LOCAL AND NATIONAL WINES